CHRISTMAS FAVORITES
for Mandolin

Arranged by Jim Schustedt

ISBN-13: 978-1-4234-1399-8

HAL•LEONARD®
CORPORATION

7777 W. BLUEMOUND RD. P.O. BOX 13819 MILWAUKEE, WI 53213

In Australia Contact:
Hal Leonard Australia Pty. Ltd.
4 Lentara Court
Cheltenham, Victoria, 3192 Australia
Email: ausadmin@halleonard.com

Visit Hal Leonard Online at
www.halleonard.com

Blue Christmas

Words and Music by Billy Hayes and Jay Johnson

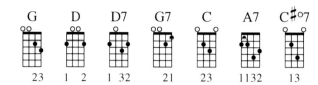

Verse

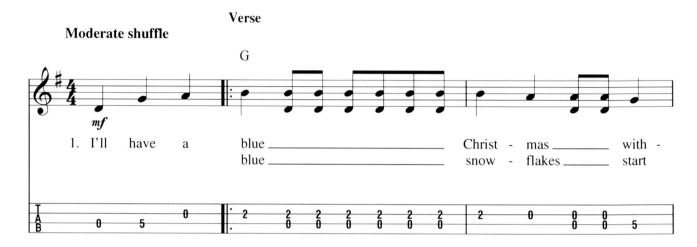

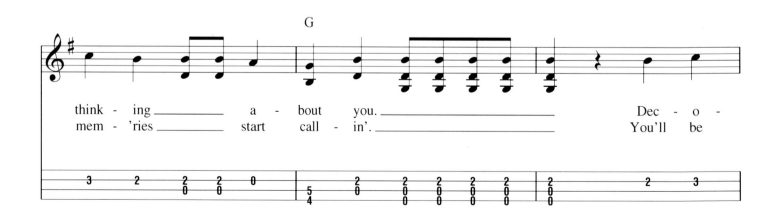

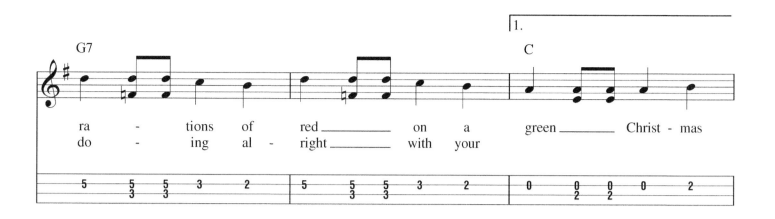

ra - tions of red _____ on a green _____ Christ - mas
do - ing al - right _____ with your

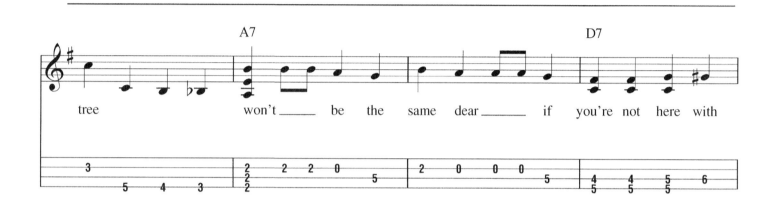

tree won't _____ be the same dear _____ if you're not here with

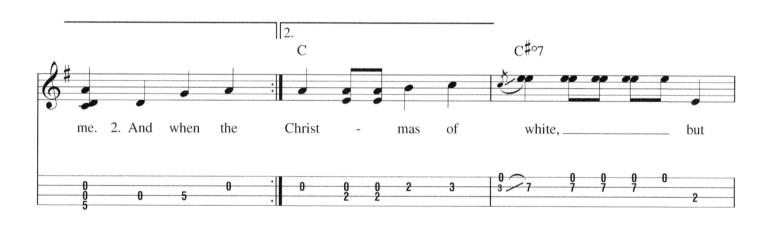

me. 2. And when the Christ - mas of white, _____ but

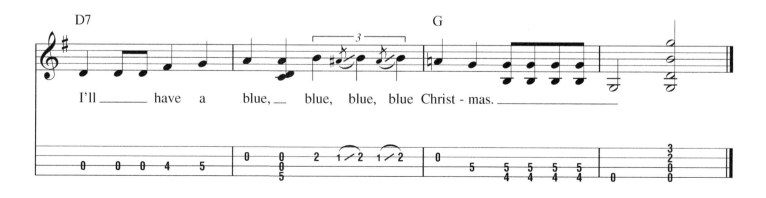

I'll _____ have a blue, __ blue, blue, blue Christ - mas. _____

Christmas in Dixie

Words and Music by Jeffrey Cook, Teddy Gentry, Mark Herndon and Randy Owen

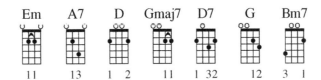

Intro
Moderately

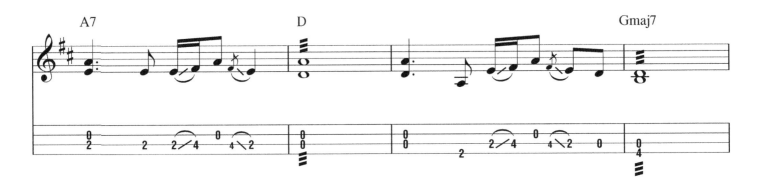

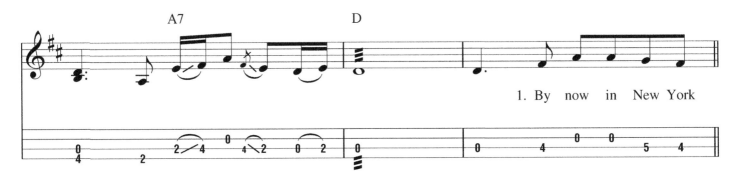

1. By now in New York

Verse

Cit - y, _____ there's snow on the ground.
ca - go, _____ the kids are out of school.

Pitch: D

*Strike the note while the fret-hand lightly
 touches the string directly over the 5th fret.

5

pines. Mer - ry Christ - mas from Dix - ie, _____

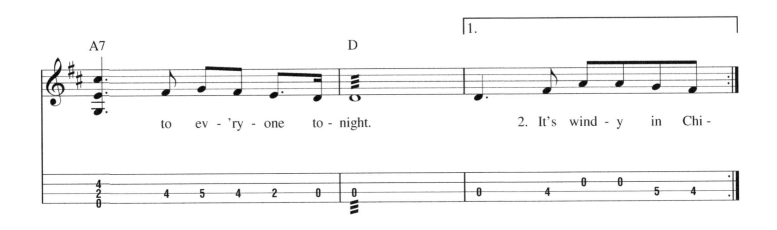

to ev - 'ry - one to - night. 2. It's wind - y in Chi -

And from Fort Payne, Al - a - bam - a, _____ Mer - ry Christ-mas to -

Slowly

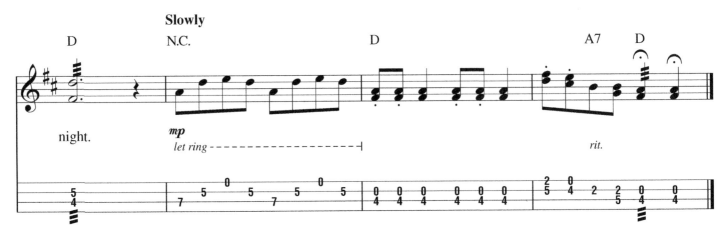

night. *mp*

let ring - *rit.*

Frosty the Snow Man

Words and Music by Steve Nelson and Jack Rollins

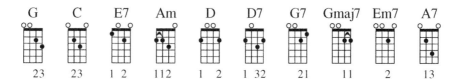

Verse
Brightly

1. Frost - y, the snow man was a jol - ly hap - py
3. Frost - y, the snow man knew the sun was hot that

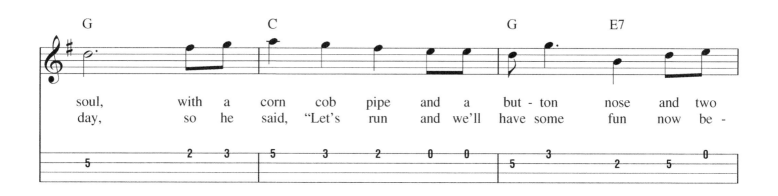

soul, with a corn cob pipe and a but - ton nose and two
day, so he said, "Let's run and we'll have some fun now be -

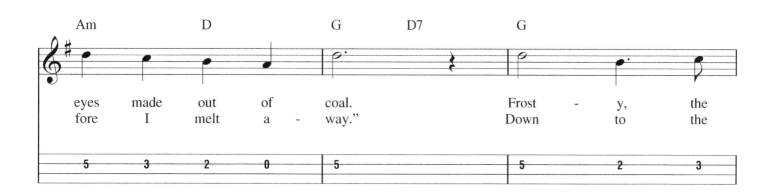

eyes made out of coal. Frost - y, the
fore I melt a - way." Down to the

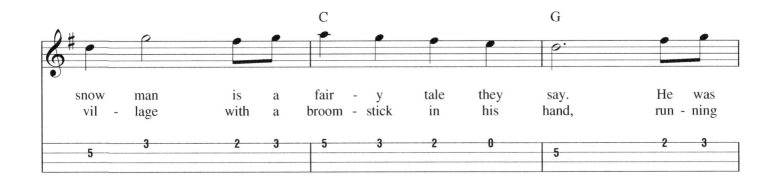

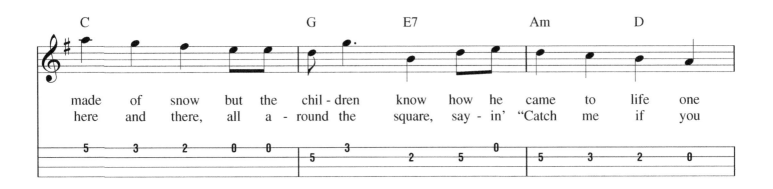

Bridge

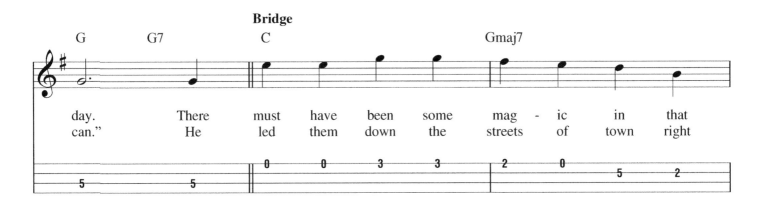

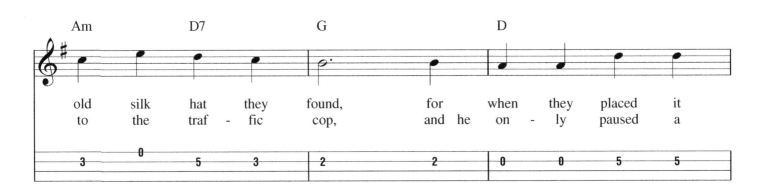

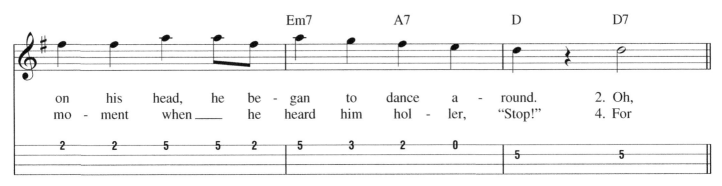

Verse

G

Frost - y, the snow man was a - live as he could
Frost - y, the snow man had to hur - ry on his

G   C   G   E7

be,   and the chil - dren say   he could laugh and   play   just the
way,   but he waved good - bye, say - in', "Don't you cry,   I'll be

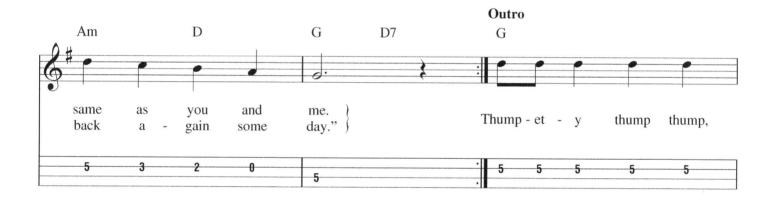

Am   D   G   D7   G

Outro

same   as   you   and   me.
back   a - gain some day."

Thump - et - y   thump thump,

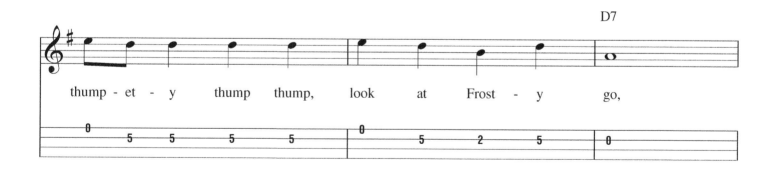

D7

thump - et - y   thump thump,   look   at   Frost - y   go,

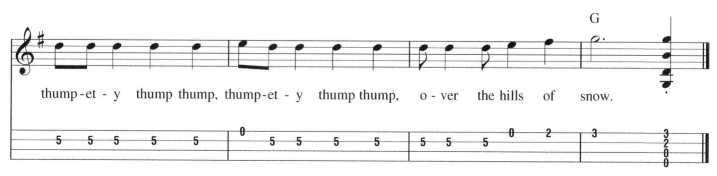

G

thump-et - y thump thump, thump-et - y thump thump, o - ver the hills of snow.

The Christmas Song
(Chestnuts Roasting on an Open Fire)

Music and Lyric by Mel Torme and Robert Wells

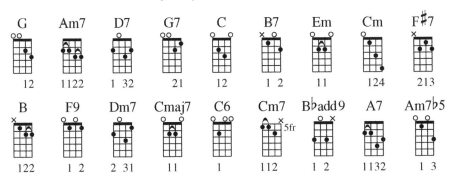

Verse

Moderately slow

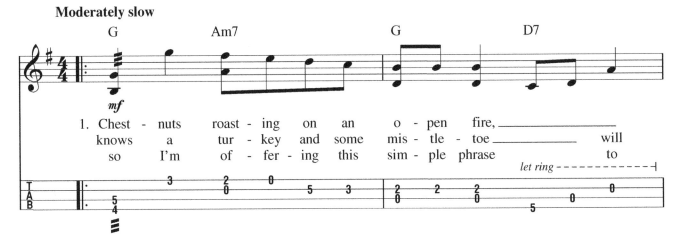

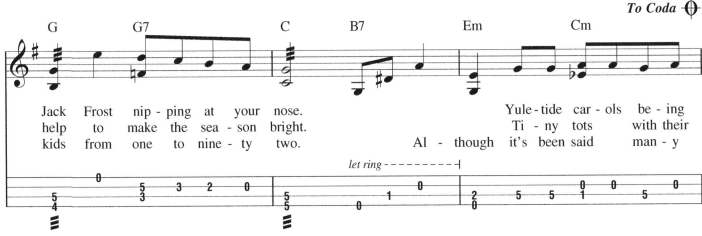

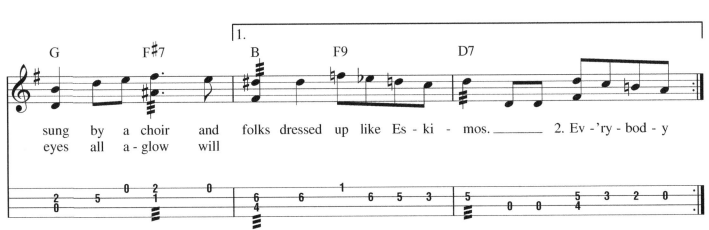

Christmas Time Is Here

from A CHARLIE BROWN CHRISTMAS

Words by Lee Mendelson
Music by Vince Guaraldi

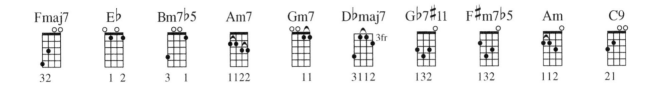

Verse

Slowly

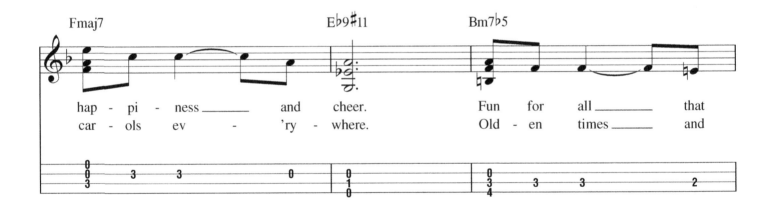

Bridge

Outro-Verse

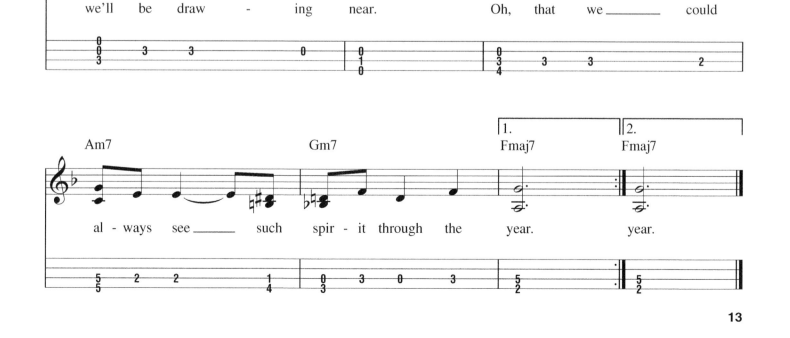

Do You Hear What I Hear

Words and Music by Noel Regney and Gloria Shayne

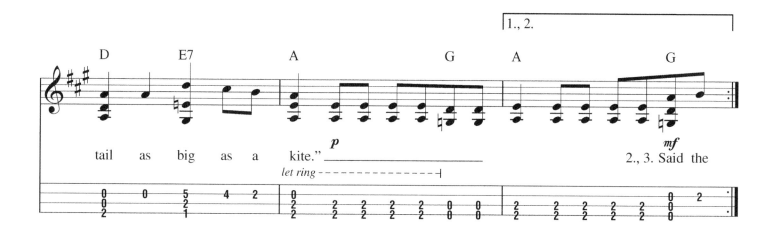

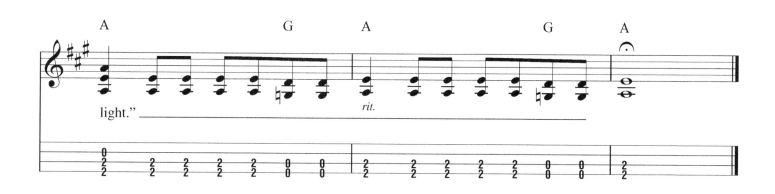

Additional Lyrics

2. Said the little lamb to the shepherd boy,
   "Do you hear what I hear?
   Ringing through the sky, shepherd boy,
   Do you hear what I hear?
   A song, a song, high above the tree,
   With a voice as big as the sea,
   With a voice as big as the sea."

3. Said the shepherd boy to the mighty king,
   "Do you know what I know?
   In your palace warm, mighty king,
   Do you know what I know?
   A Child, a Child shivers in the cold,
   Let us bring him silver and gold,
   Let us bring him silver and gold."

4. Said the king to the people ev'rywhere,
   "Listen to what I say!
   Pray for peace, people ev'rywhere,
   Listen to what I say!
   The Child, the Child, sleeping in the night;
   He will bring us goodness and light,
   He will bring us goodness and light."

Here Comes Santa Claus
(Right Down Santa Claus Lane)

Words and Music by Gene Autry and Oakley Haldeman

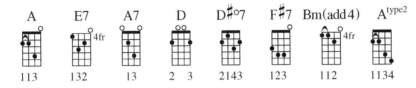

Verse
Moderately

1. Here comes San - ta Claus! Here comes San - ta Claus! Right down San - ta Claus
2., 3., 4. *See additional lyrics*

Lane!   Vix - en and Blit - zen and all his rein - deer are

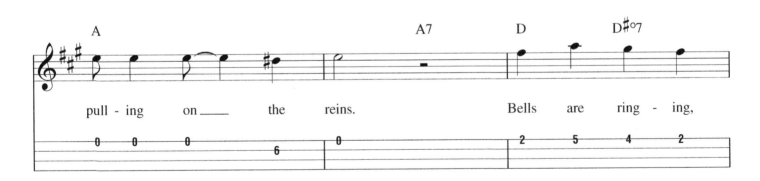

pull - ing on ___ the reins.   Bells are ring - ing,

chil - dren sing - ing, all is mer - ry and bright.

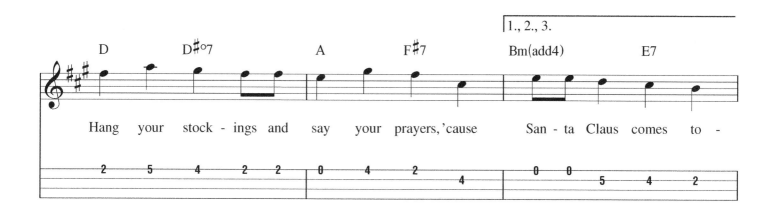

Hang your stock - ings and say your prayers, 'cause San - ta Claus comes to -

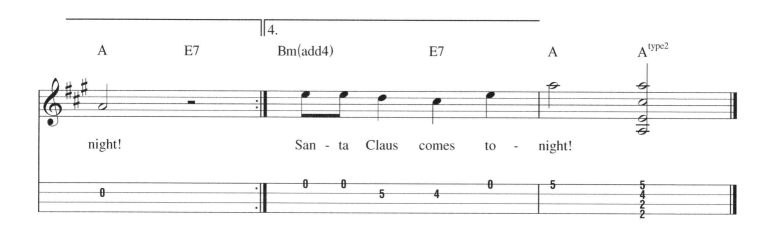

night! San - ta Claus comes to - night!

Additional Lyrics

2. Here comes Santa Claus! Here comes Santa Claus!
   Right down Santa Claus Lane!
   He's got a bag that is filled with toys
   For the boys and girls again.
   Hear those sleigh bells jingle, jangle,
   What a beautiful sight.
   Jump in bed, cover up your head,
   Santa Claus comes tonight.

3. Here comes Santa Claus! Here comes Santa Claus!
   Right down Santa Claus Lane!
   He doesn't care if you're rich or poor,
   For he loves you just the same.
   Santa knows that we're God's children;
   That makes ev'rything right.
   Fill your hearts with a Christmas cheer,
   'Cause Santa Claus comes tonight.

4. Here comes Santa Claus! Here comes Santa Claus!
   Right down Santa Claus Lane!
   He'll come around when the chimes ring out;
   Then it's Christmas morn again.
   Peace on earth will come to all
   If we just follow the light
   Let's give thanks to the Lord above,
   Santa Claus comes tonight.

A Holly Jolly Christmas

Music and Lyrics by Johnny Marks

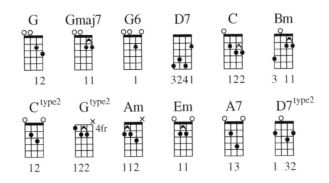

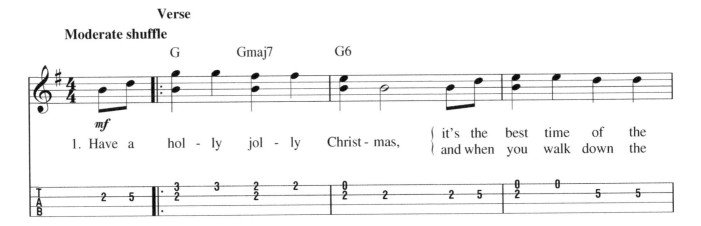

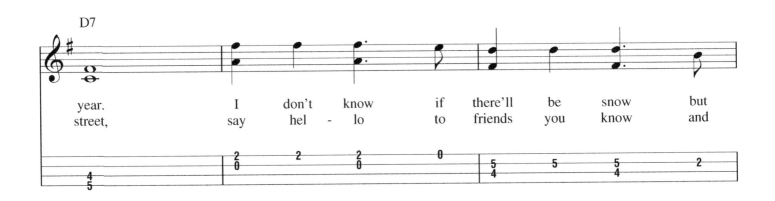

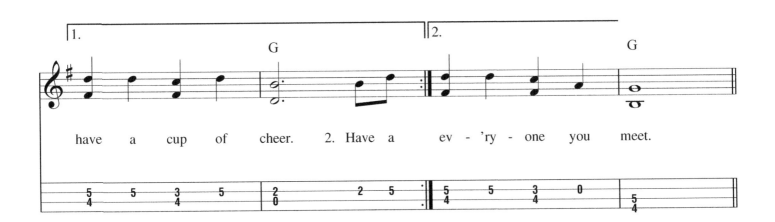

Bridge

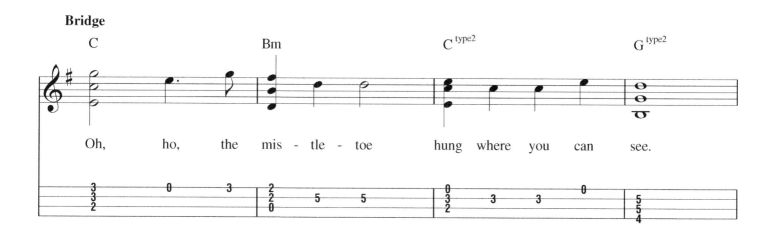

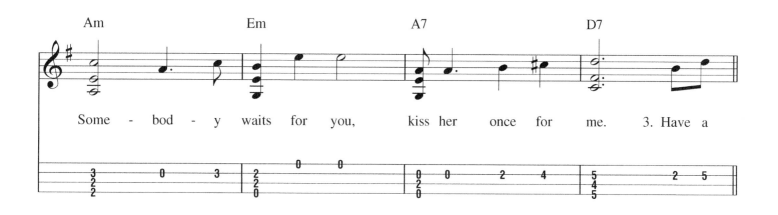

Outro - Verse

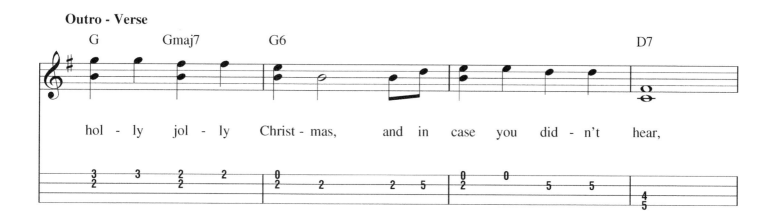

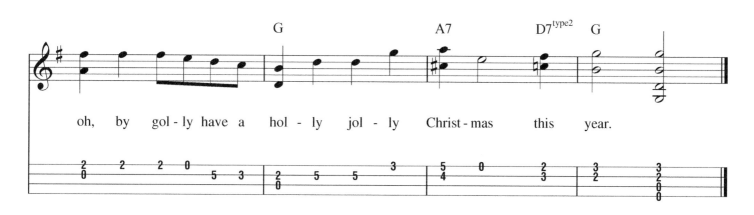

I Saw Mommy Kissing Santa Claus

Words and Music by Tommie Connor

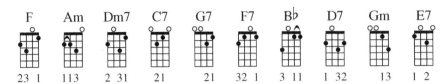

Verse
Moderately

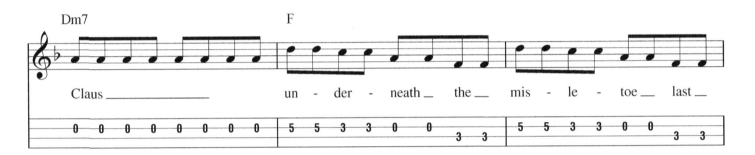

I _____ saw ___ Mom - my ___ kiss - ing ___ San - ta ___

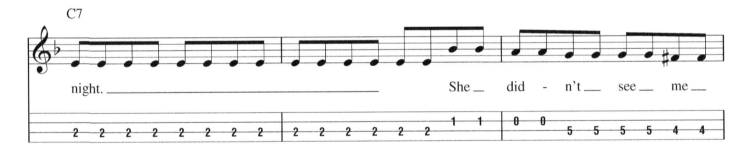

Claus _____ un - der - neath ___ the ___ mis - le - toe ___ last ___

night. _____ She ___ did - n't ___ see ___ me ___

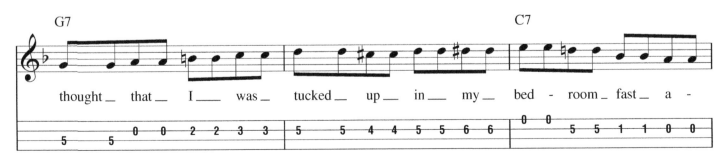

creep _____ down the stairs ___ to ___ have ___ a ___ peep. _____ She ___

thought ___ that ___ I ___ was ___ tucked up ___ in ___ my ___ bed - room ___ fast ___ a -

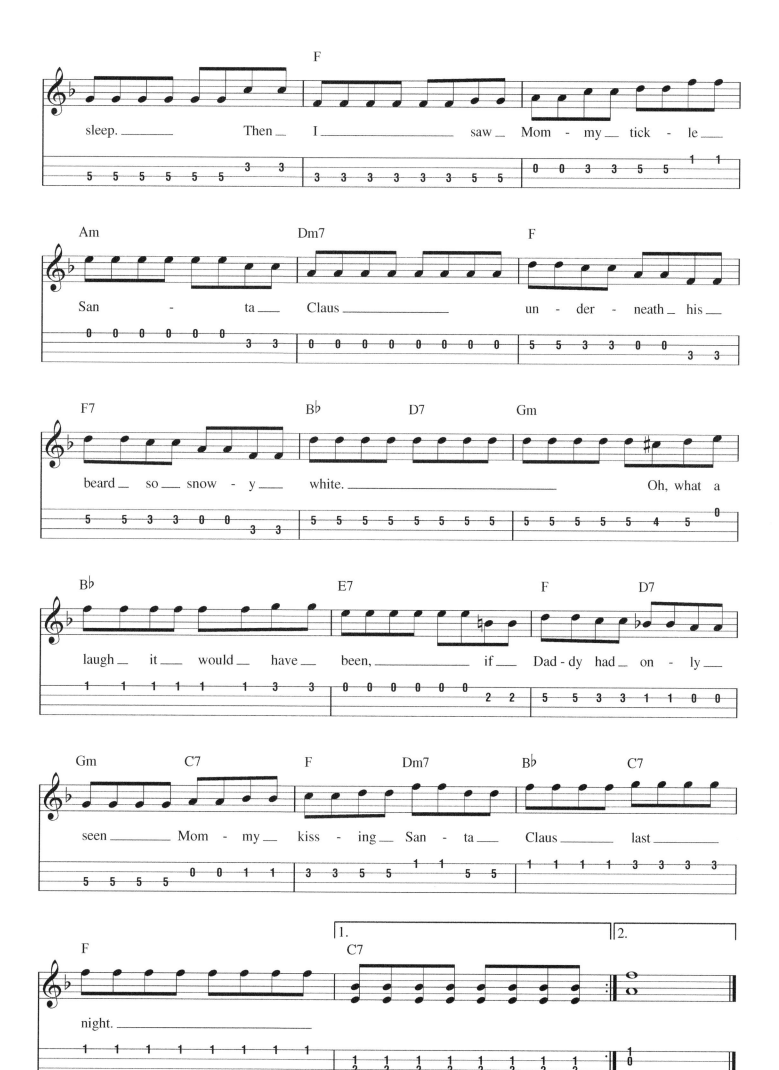

I'll Be Home for Christmas

Words and Music by Kim Gannon and Walter Kent

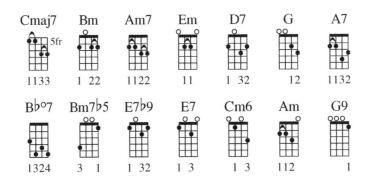

Intro
Moderately slow

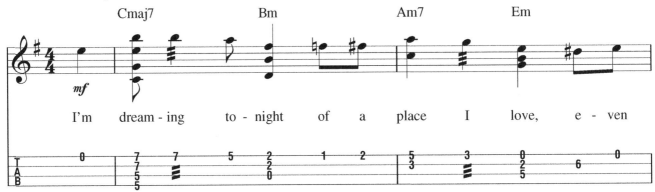

I'm dream-ing to-night of a place I love, e-ven

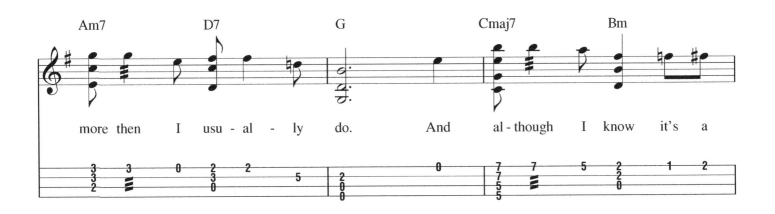

more then I usu-al-ly do. And al-though I know it's a

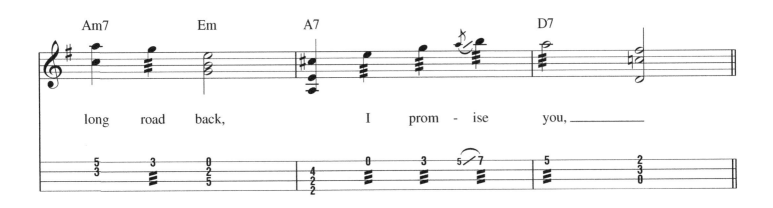

long road back, I prom-ise you, _____

Verse

1. I'll   be   home   for   Christ -   mas, _____

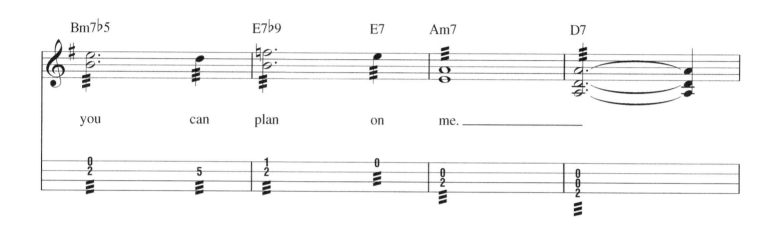

you   can   plan   on   me. _____

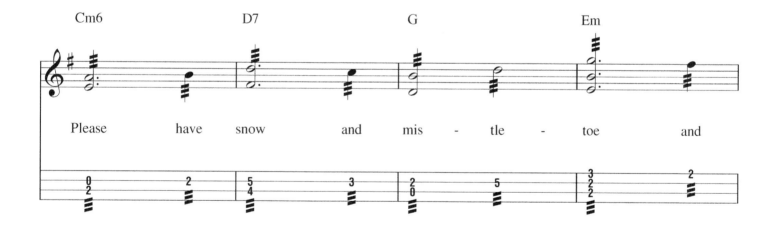

Please   have   snow   and   mis - tle - toe   and

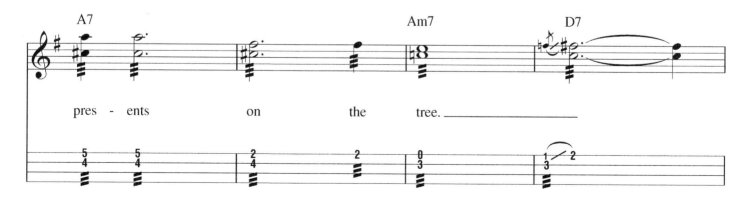

pres - ents   on   the   tree. _____

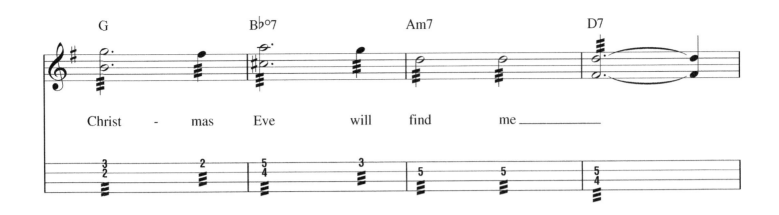

Christ - mas Eve will find me

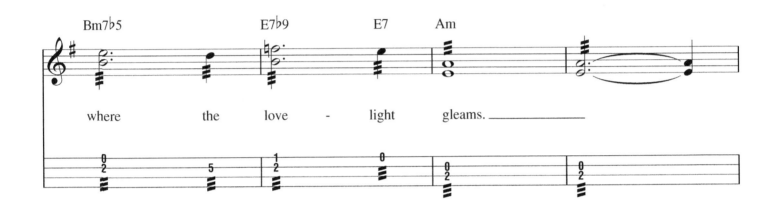

where the love - light gleams.

I'll be home for Christ - mas if

on - ly in my dreams.

Jingle-Bell Rock

Words and Music by Joe Beal and Jim Boothe

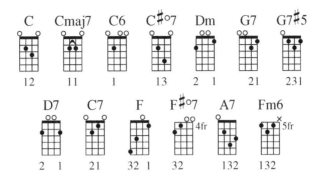

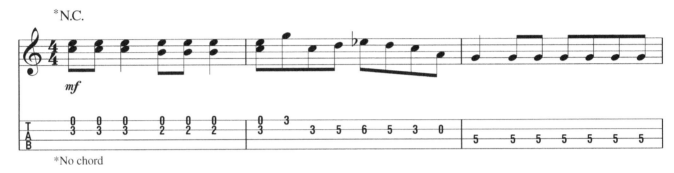

Intro

Moderate shuffle

*N.C.

*No chord

𝄋 Verse

1., 3. Jin - gle - bell, jin - gle - bell,

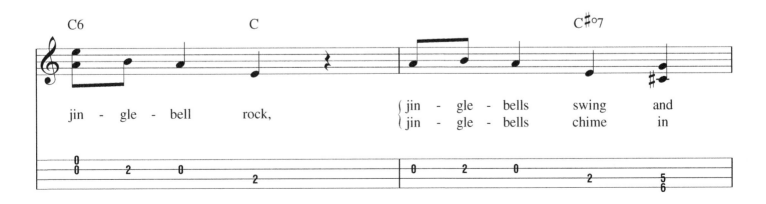

jin - gle - bell rock, { jin - gle - bells swing and
{ jin - gle - bells chime in

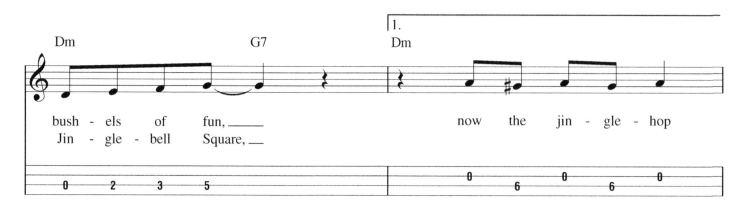

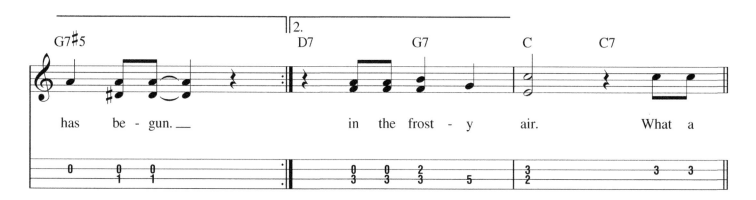

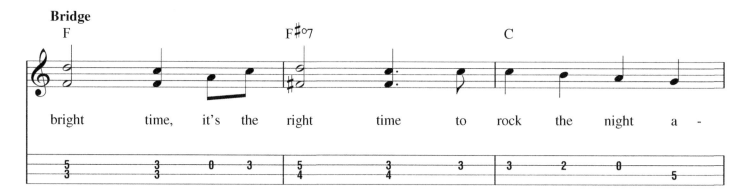

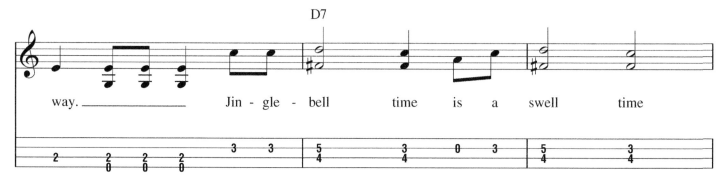

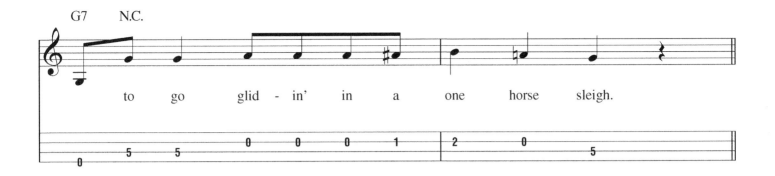

to go glid - in' in a one horse sleigh.

Outro-Verse

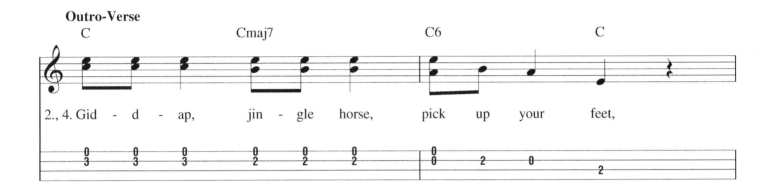

2., 4. Gid - d - ap, jin - gle horse, pick up your feet,

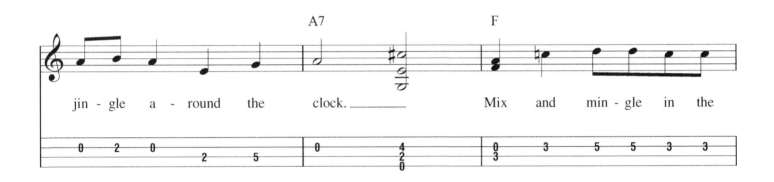

jin - gle a - round the clock. _____ Mix and min - gle in the

To Coda ⊕   *D.S. al Coda*
(take repeat)

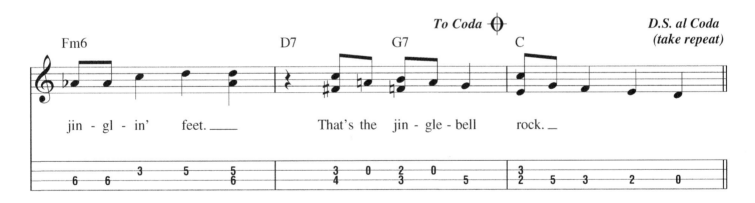

jin - gl - in' feet. _____ That's the jin - gle - bell rock. __

⊕ **Coda**

that's the jin - gle - bell, that's the jin - gle - bell rock.

Let It Snow! Let It Snow! Let It Snow!

Words by Sammy Cahn
Music by Jule Styne

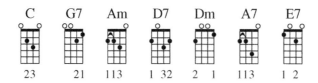

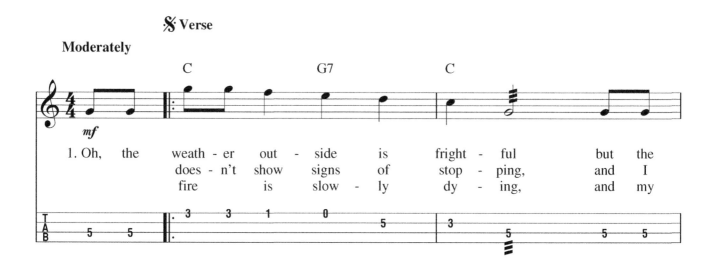

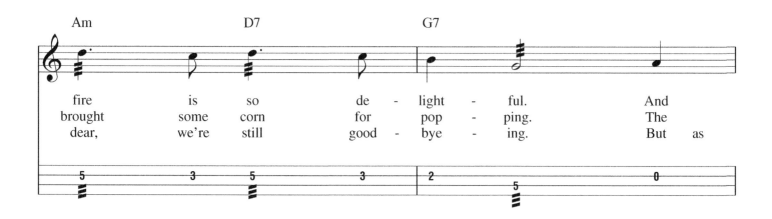

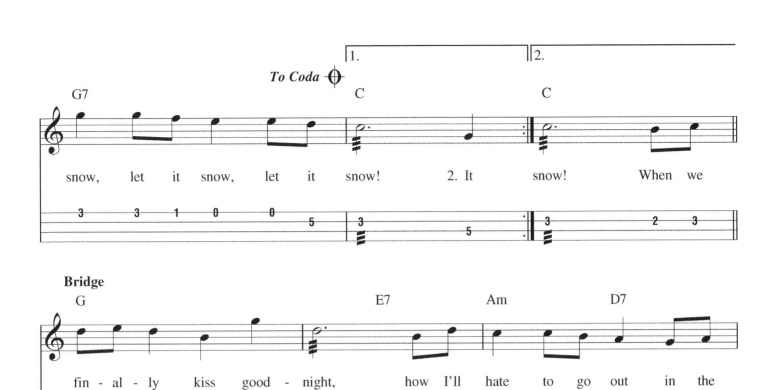

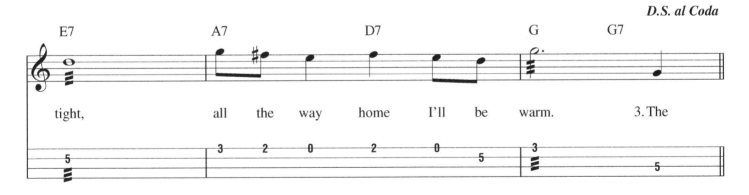

from Carpenters – *Christmas Portrait*

Merry Christmas, Darling

Words and Music by Richard Carpenter and Frank Pooler

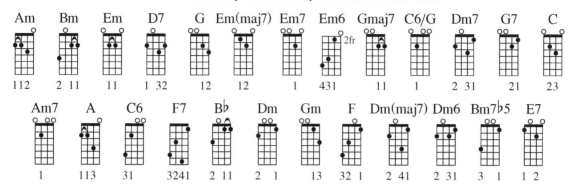

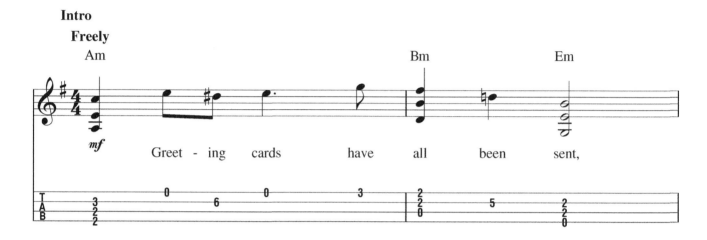

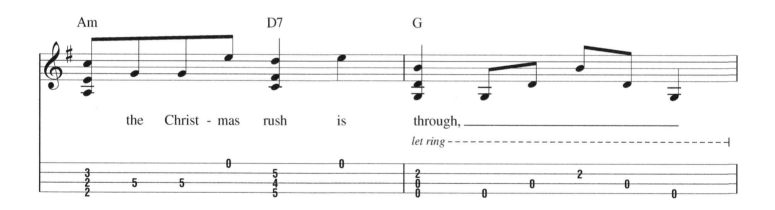

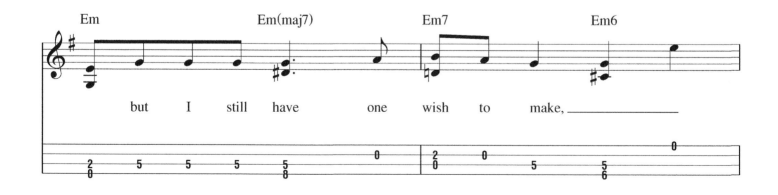

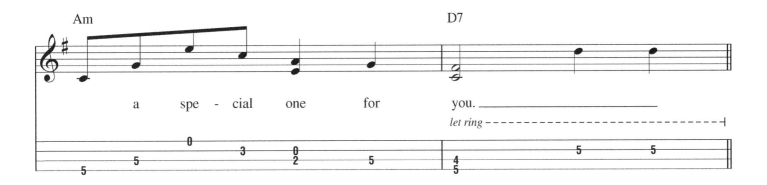

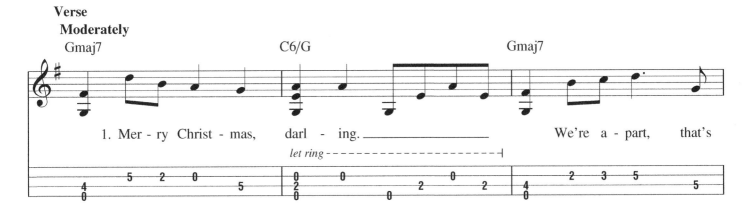

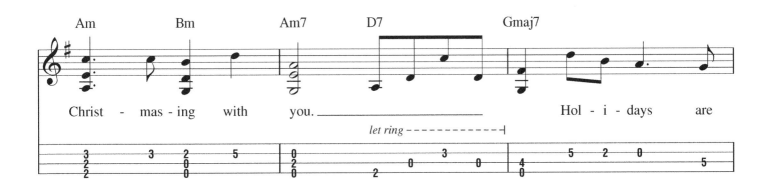

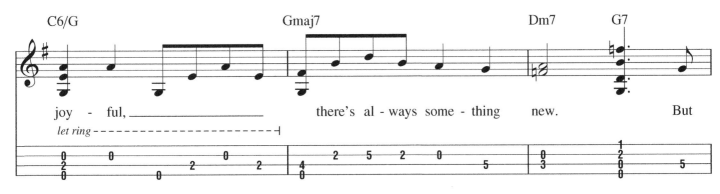

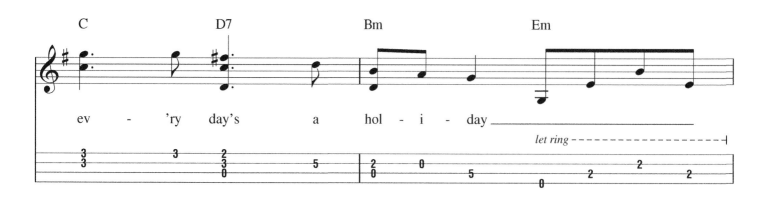

ev - 'ry day's a hol - i - day _____

let ring - - - - - - - - - - - - - - -

% **Bridge**

when I'm near to you. _____ The __ lights on the tree I

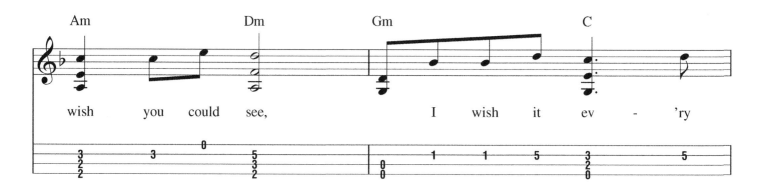

wish you could see, I wish it ev - 'ry

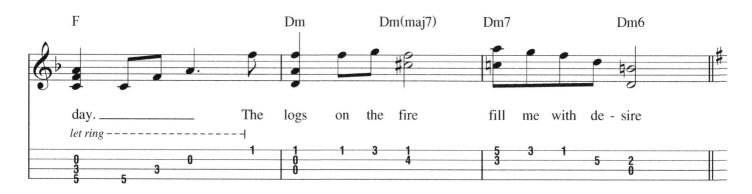

day. _____ The logs on the fire fill me with de - sire

let ring - - - - - - - - - - - -

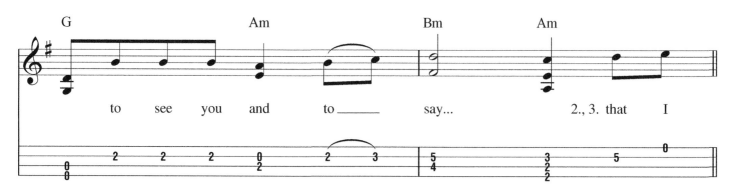

to see you and to _____ say... 2., 3. that I

My Favorite Things

from THE SOUND OF MUSIC

Lyrics by Oscar Hammerstein II
Music by Richard Rodgers

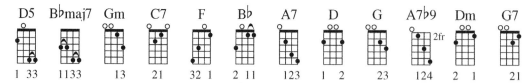

Verse
Moderately slow

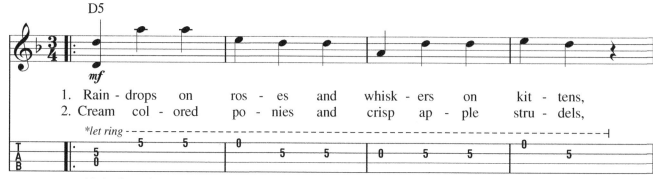

1. Rain-drops on ros-es and whisk-ers on kit-tens,
2. Cream col-ored po-nies and crisp ap-ple stru-dels,

*let ring

*3rd string only

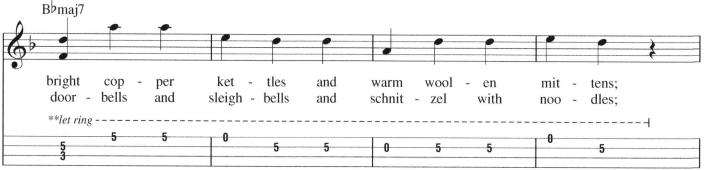

bright cop-per ket-tles and warm wool-en mit-tens;
door-bells and sleigh-bells and schnit-zel with noo-dles;

**let ring

**3rd string only

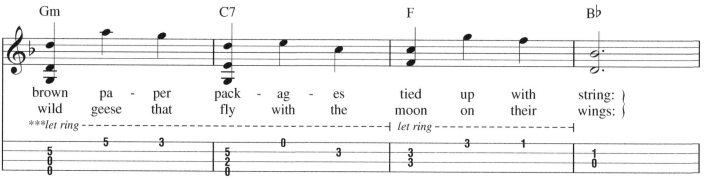

brown pa-per pack-ag-es tied up with string: }
wild geese that fly with the moon on their wings: }

***let ring   let ring

***3rd & 4th strings only

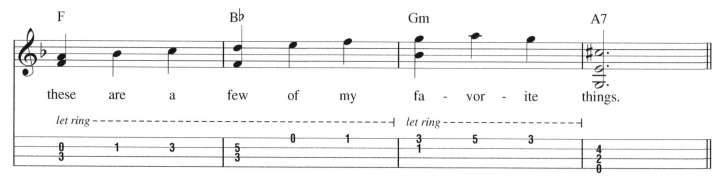

these are a few of my fa-vor-ite things.

let ring   let ring

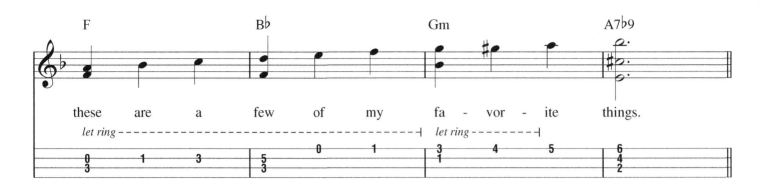

these are a few of my fa - vor - ite things.

Outro

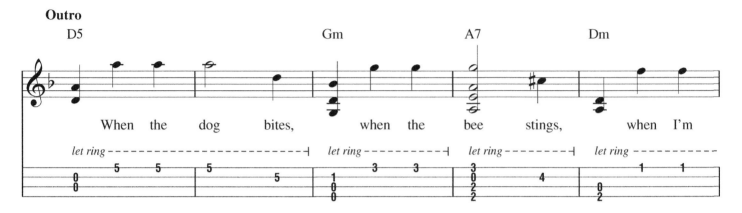

When the dog bites, when the bee stings, when I'm

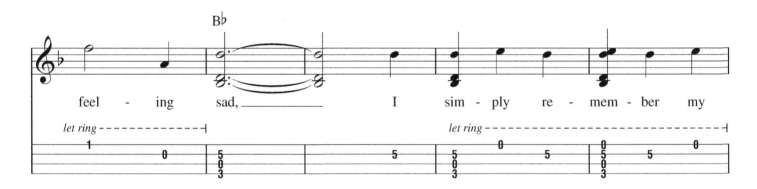

feel - ing sad, _____ I sim - ply re - mem - ber my

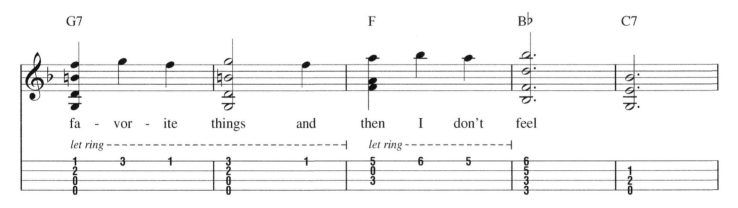

fa - vor - ite things and then I don't feel

so bad. _____

Rudolph the Red-Nosed Reindeer

Music and Lyrics by Johnny Marks

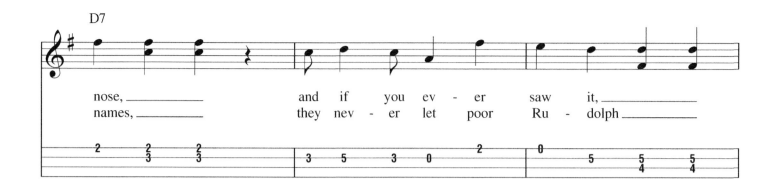

Bridge

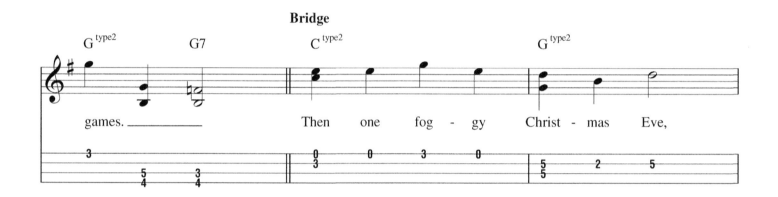

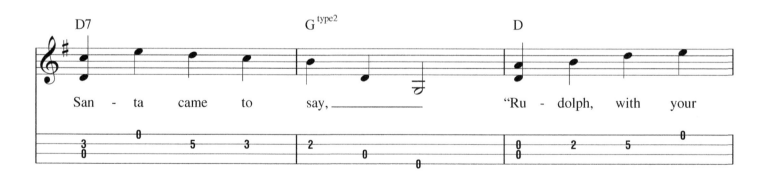

Outro - Verse

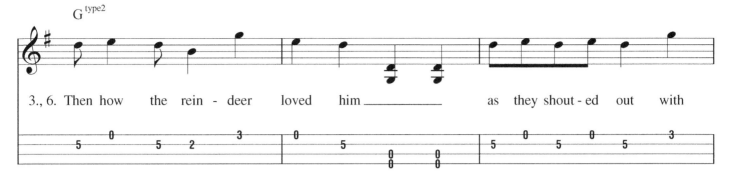

3., 6. Then how the rein - deer loved him _____ as they shout - ed out with

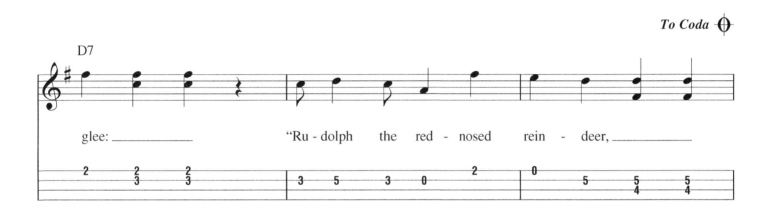

To Coda ⊕

glee: _____ "Ru - dolph the red - nosed rein - deer, _____

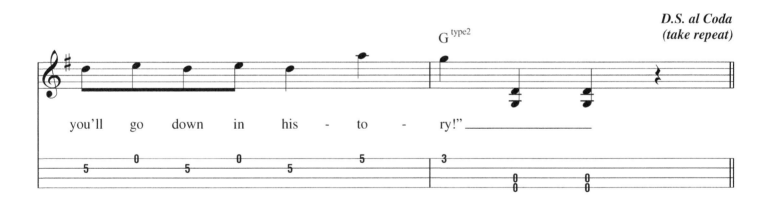

D.S. al Coda
(take repeat)

you'll go down in his - to - ry!" _____

 Coda

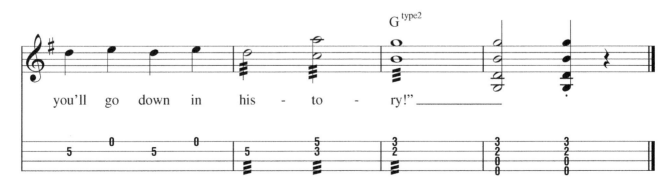

you'll go down in his - to - ry!" _____

Rockin' Around the Christmas Tree

Music and Lyrics by Johnny Marks

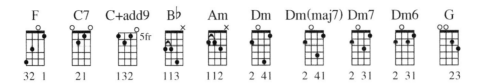

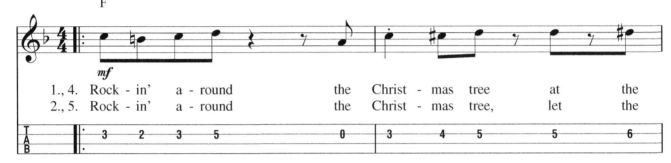

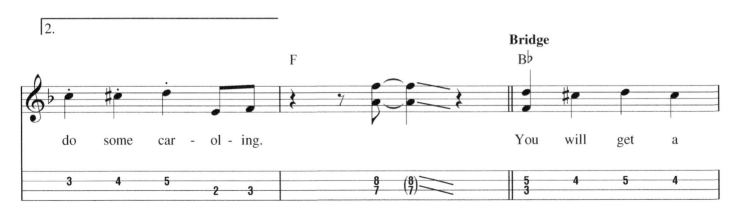

sen - ti - men - tal   feel - ing   when   you   hear

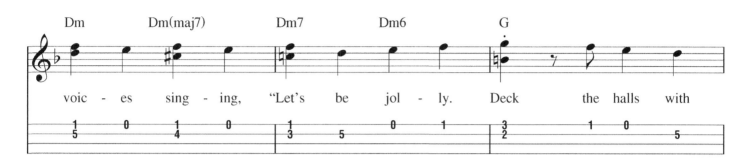

voic - es   sing - ing,   "Let's   be   jol - ly.   Deck   the   halls   with

Outro-Verse

boughs   of   hol - ly."   3., 6. Rock - in'   a - round   the   Christ - mas tree,   have   a

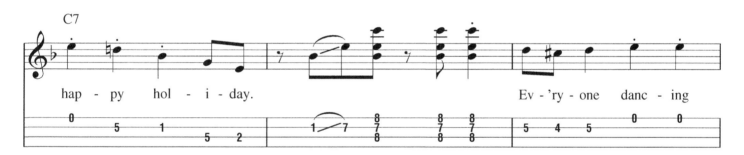

hap - py   hol - i - day.   Ev - 'ry - one   danc - ing

To Coda ⊕   *D.C. al Coda*
(take repeat)

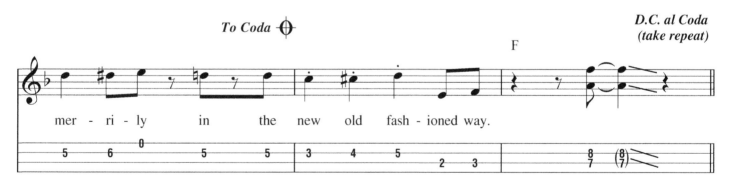

mer - ri - ly   in   the   new   old   fash - ioned way.

⊕ **Coda**

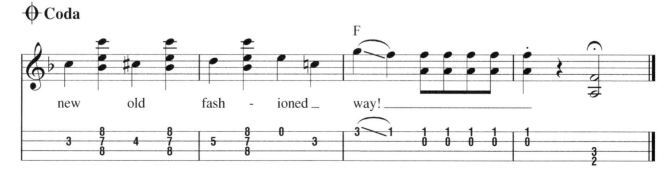

new   old   fash - ioned _ way! _____

Santa Claus Is Comin' to Town

Words by Haven Gillespie
Music by J. Fred Coots

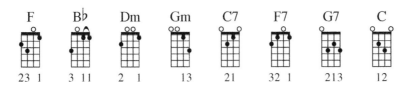

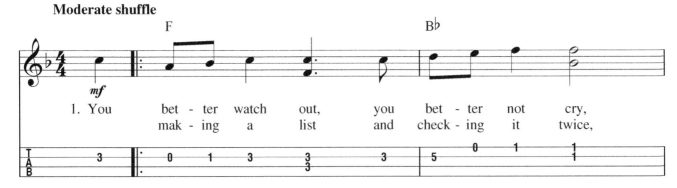

Verse

Moderate shuffle

1. You bet - ter watch out, you bet - ter not cry,
   mak - ing a list and check - ing it twice,

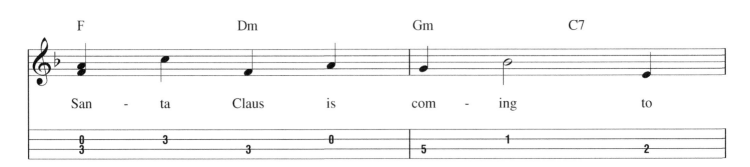

bet - ter not pout, I'm tell - ing you why: }
gon - na find out who's naugh - ty and nice. }

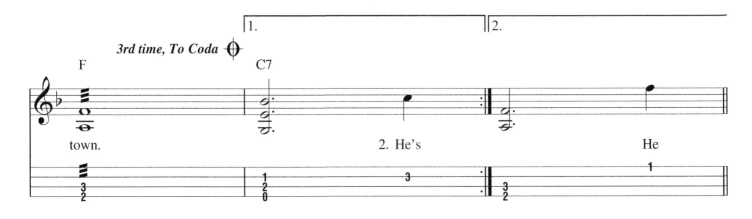

San - ta Claus is com - ing to

3rd time, To Coda

town.   2. He's   He

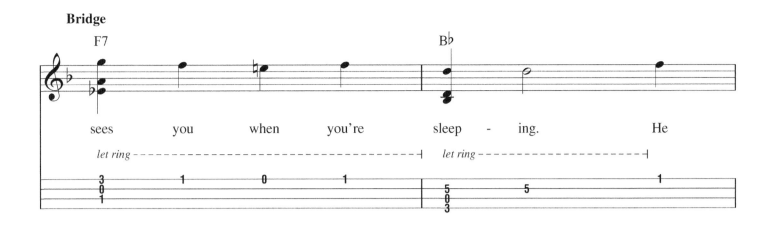

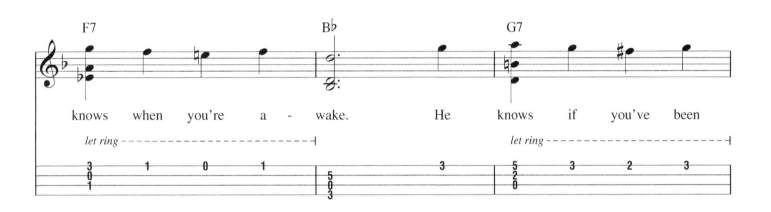

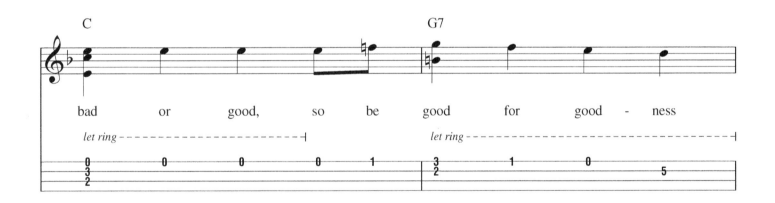

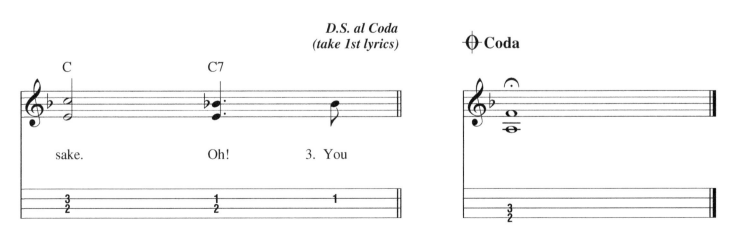

Bridge

F7 ... sees you when you're sleep - ing. He
Bb

F7 ... knows when you're a - wake. He knows if you've been
Bb ... G7

C ... bad or good, so be good for good - ness
G7

D.S. al Coda
(take 1st lyrics)

⊕ **Coda**

C ... sake. Oh! 3. You
C7

43

Silver Bells

from the Paramount Picture THE LEMON DROP KID

Words and Music by Jay Livingston and Ray Evans

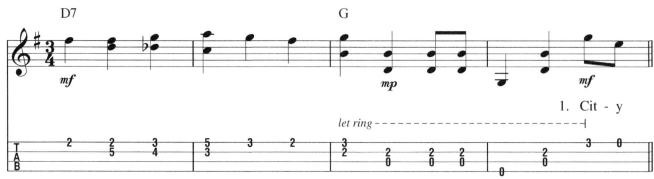

Intro
Moderately

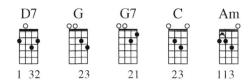

1. Cit - y

Verse

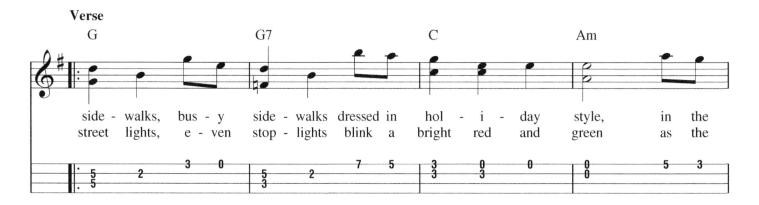

side - walks, bus - y side - walks dressed in hol - i - day style, in the
street lights, e - ven stop - lights blink a bright red and green as the

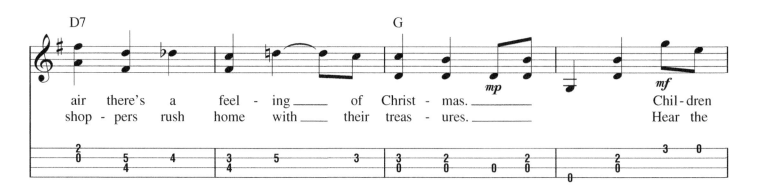

air there's a feel - ing _____ of Christ - mas. Chil - dren
shop - pers rush home with _____ their treas - ures. _____ Hear the

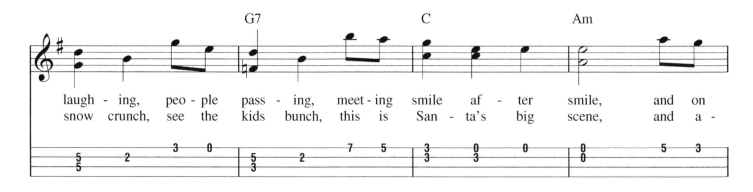

laugh - ing, peo - ple pass - ing, meet - ing smile af - ter smile, and on
snow crunch, see the kids bunch, this is San - ta's big scene, and a -

You're All I Want for Christmas

Words and Music by Glen Moore and Seger Ellis

Mandolin Notation Legend

Mandolin music can be notated three different ways: on a *musical staff*, in *tablature*, and in *rhythm slashes*.

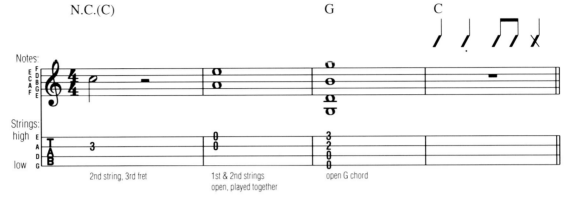

RHYTHM SLASHES are written above the staff. Strum chords in the rhythm indicated. Use the chord diagrams found at the top of the first page of the transcription for the appropriate chord voicings.

THE MUSICAL STAFF shows pitches and rhythms and is divided by bar lines into measures. Pitches are named after the first seven letters of the alphabet.

TABLATURE graphically represents the mandolin fretboard. Each of the four horizontal lines represents each of the four courses of strings, and each number represents a fret.

Definitions for Special Mandolin Notation

MUTED STRING(S): Lightly touch a string with the edge of your fret-hand finger while fretting a note on an adjacent string, causing the muted string to be unheard. Muting all of the strings with the fingers of the fret-hand while strumming the strings with the picking hand produces a percussive effect.

HAMMER-ON: Strike the first (lower) note with one finger, then sound the higher note (on the same string) with another finger by fretting it without picking.

PULL-OFF: Place both fingers on the notes to be sounded. Strike the first note and, without picking, pull the finger off to sound the second (lower) note.

LEGATO SLIDE: Strike the first note and then slide the same fret-hand finger up or down to the second note. The second note is not struck.

SHIFT SLIDE: Same as the legato slide except the second note is struck.

HALF-STEP BEND: Strike the note and bend up ½ step.

GRACE NOTE BEND: Strike the note and immediately bend up as indicated.

TREMOLO PICKING: The note is picked rapidly and continuously.

Additional Musical Definitions

_p_ *(piano)*	• Play quietly.
_mp_ *(mezzo-piano)*	• Play moderately quiet.
_mf_ *(mezzo-forte)*	• Play moderately loud.
_f_ *(forte)*	• Play loudly.
cont. rhy. sim.	• Continue strumming in similar rhythm.
N.C. *(no chord)*	• Don't strum until the next chord symbol. Chord symbols in parentheses reflect implied harmony.
D.S. al Coda	• Go back to the sign (%), then play until the measure marked *"To Coda"*, then skip to the section labeled **"Coda."**
D.S.S. al Coda 2	• Go back to the double sign (%%), then play until the measure marked *"To Coda 2"*, then skip to the section labeled **"Coda 2."**
D.S. al Fine	• Go back to the sign (%), then play until the label *"Fine."*

 *(staccato)* • Play the note or chord short.

 (ritard) • Gradually slow down.

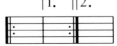 *(fermata)* • Hold the note or chord for an undetermined amount of time.

• Repeat measures between signs.

1. 2. • When a repeated section has different endings, play the first ending only the first time and the second ending only the second time.

NOTE: Tablature numbers in parentheses mean:
1. The note is being sustained over a system (note in standard notation is tied), or
2. The note is sustained, but a new articulation (such as a hammer-on, pull-off or slide) begins.

48